Remember Chesham

Portrait of a Country Town

For Carolyn,

grand-daughter of Augustus Writer.

A country town. (W)

REMEMBER CHESHAM

Portrait of a Country Town

by

Clive Birch

with additional photography by

John Armistead

BARRACUDA BOOKS LIMITED
BUCKINGHAM, ENGLAND
MCMLXXIX

PUBLISHED BY BARRACUDA BOOKS LIMITED
BUCKINGHAM, ENGLAND
DESIGNED BY CALYPUS DESIGN OF BUCKINGHAM
AND PRINTED BY
BUSIPRINT LIMITED OF BUCKINGHAM

BOUND BY DOLPHIN DISTRIBUTION LTD
OF AYLESBURY, ENGLAND

LITHOGRAPHY, AND TEXT SET IN
TIMES ROMAN
BY BRIAN ROBINSON OF
NORTH MARSTON, ENGLAND

ISBN 0 86023 107 0

Contents

Writer's Chesham

In recent years, like many towns within the Metropolitan belt, Chesham in Buckinghamshire has seen much physical change — new housing developments, traffic intensified by motorways, rail link electrified, stores replacing shops, and a new generation of public buildings. Yet one can still stand in the town centre and see green hills on every side.

Perhaps it is the resilience of a community with its roots in prehistory, its industrial origins in Saxon times and its record of nonconformity which prompts a healthy appetite for records of the past. Certainly, its essential character has not altered over much — incomers have not changed Chesham; it changes them. Perhaps it is simply typical of England's smaller country towns — aware of their traditions, proud of their shared heritage.

Whatever the reason, this town welcomed first the *Book of Chesham* in 1974, and then *Yesterday's Town: Chesham,* three years later. Since then local people have asked for some record of the early decades of our own century. This book attempts to reflect this town and others like it in the Edwardian era and after — a selective portrait of place, people and events within living memory.

Communities like Chesham have been lucky in their early photographers — there are still many hundreds of unpublished pictures. Yet something more was needed when first this book was planned in 1978. Recently a hitherto unknown collection of several hundred photographs of the period c1915-1925 came into my hands. An *Observer* photographer who saw them thought they were pure magic. The photographer was a Chesham businessman, originally from Kennington, London, and if his shots of the town are unusual, his studies of his children are exceptional.

That man was Augustus Writer. This book largely represents Writer's Chesham. He helped to run the family leather warehouse in Red Lion Street, and whenever something caught his eye, he recorded it. Of course, many of the pictures are by other hands and I acknowledge my debt to them all, and especially to the town's contemporary photographer, John Armistead, who reshot many of the faded originals. I am also grateful to all who responded to my appeal for additional material.

My primary acknowledgement must be to Augustus Writer's family, for allowing me access to their albums, and permission to reproduce their portraits.

In the end, this book owes its appeal and much of its content to Writer. I have taken his studies of his five children in all their moods and activities, to highlight each selection, to unfold the record of streets, people and events from the turn of the century to the early '30s. It is the children who lead us down the hills, through the town and into its heart. I hope they take you into their hearts as they did me, and that with them you may remember Chesham, in this portrait of a country town.

Remember Chesham

Chesham — a Chiltern town, backed by beechwoods and framed by field and tree. (W)

ABOVE: Before they built houses in Lowndes Avenue, we played on the Co-op Field, (W) and BELOW: in those days Bois Moor Road had a positively rural aspect.

LEFT: Long gone Townfield was one of Chesham's small, if squalid alleys, (W) and RIGHT: Germain Street before the cinema came in 1936; BELOW: Gossips met in Church Street.

My Lords, Ladies...

ABOVE: Back from the Boers, 1901, and BELOW: long live King George the Fifth, June 22, 1911.

Off to School

ABOVE: Townsend Road Girls' School, class of '18. (G) CENTRE: Hats on for the Sunday School fête at The Bury, in the '20s. (W) BELOW: Out of school, by The Forelands, Baptist ministerial residence. (Note the wooden hoop — a local product.) (W)

Making Good

ABOVE: Clearing the cressbeds, a traditional cottage industry: Red Lion Street where the Mead water gardens are now. (W) LEFT: Chilterns woodwork: Jesse Moulder at Easts's in Fuller's Hill. (WTM) RIGHT: Woman's work: Great Aunt Bessie Peasland prepares a meal, Bellingdon Road. (W)

ABOVE: The workforce of a local factory, (A) and BELOW: on a building site somewhere in Chesham, both 20's. (G)

RIGHT: You had to be strong to work in Harry Wing's slaughterhouse behind the Golden Ball. (G) LEFT: Augustus Writer's warehouse in Red Lion Street. (W) BELOW: Woodworkers making beach spades, hoops and cricket bats. (D).

Uphill Downhill

Long haul through Captain's Wood. (W) INSET: Accident! (B)

ABOVE: A strange contraption outside the Doctor's house in High Street, and BELOW: no yellow lines in High Street, with Mead's waggon on the left.

ABOVE: A tight thing, entering the town by the old Red Lion by Germain Street, and BELOW: trouble for Wright's timber truck. (D)

Raising Steam

ABOVE: The Chesham shuttle at *the* platform. BELOW: Engine power down on the farm — in the Vale. (W)

Rainy Days

ABOVE: The floods of '17 at the Asheridge Road-Hivings Hill junction, (W) and LEFT: devastation at Pednor Mead. RIGHT: The rains came again — Broad Street in the '20s.

The Good Earth

ABOVE Payne's Farm, Asheridge Vale. (W) CENTRE & BELOW: Haymaking. (W)

ABOVE: Carting the crop, (W) and BELOW: elevating. (W)

ABOVE: In the rick. (W) BELOW: A well earnt drink.

Victory 1914-18

ABOVE: Explaining the tools of World War I. BELOW: Parade at the Cricket Meadow, probably Royal Engineers, Frank Howard taking the march-past. (MH)

ABOVE: Engineers relax between bouts of bridge building in the Park. BELOW: The Memorial is unveiled, 1921, in The Broadway.

ABOVE: Temporary and permanent remembrance. (W) BELOW: Veterans march down Red Lion Street. (W)

Time Off

ABOVE: What would their mothers say? (Off Church Street). (W)
BELOW: A makeshift slide at Fitzgerald's Yard in Bellingdon Road. (W)

ABOVE: Certainly a treat in store for the Broadway: here behind Red Lion Street. (W) BELOW: Having a pint outside the King's Arms in Germain Street. (G)

ABOVE: Sunday morning best outside the Cock in The Broadway, (G) and BELOW: the old One Bell, Church Street, once a tollhouse, now an off licence.

ABOVE: All dressed up to kill on a Sunday afternoon, Cow Meadows, Fullers Hill. (G) BELOW: The Griffin, Bellingdon Road.

ABOVE: The old Red Lion with distances to London (29), Uxbridge (14), Amersham (3) and Rickmansworth (9), and BELOW: the long gone Blue Ball, Blucher Street, the Reynolds' residence, also gone, behind.

Winter Sports

ABOVE: Sledging in the Park, (W) CENTRE: and by the Parish church wall. (W) BELOW: Skating in the Park.

Affairs of Moment

ABOVE: Maintaining communications at the original telephone exchange. BELOW: Postmen — and boys. (C) INSET: Joseph Reynolds, Director, Chesham and District Mutual Building Society and Secretary, 1895-1933. (M)

ABOVE: Police presence after a fire was over. BELOW: The men who fought the fires, with their wives, behind The Limes, High Street. (G)

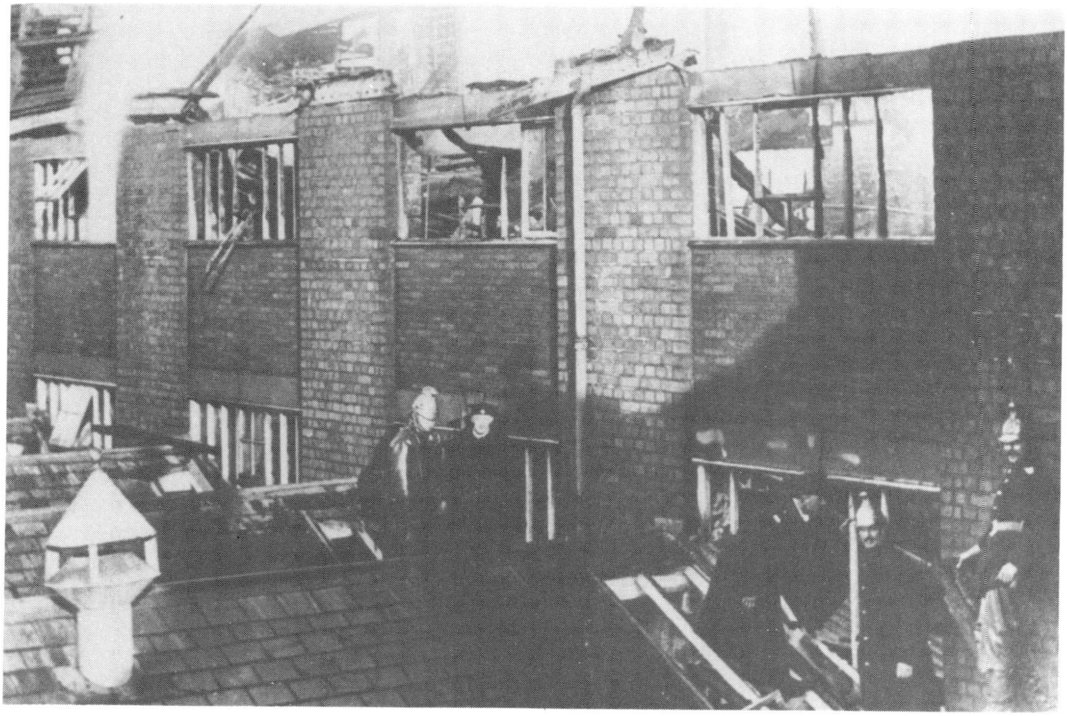

ABOVE: Beechwoods factory burnt down Saturday, March 30, 1930, 38 years after it was built. BELOW: The Brigade with 'Nora', the Leyland fire engine. Front Row l to r: R. Saunders, X, Mc Wallace, G. Robinson, R. Howard, F. Gomm, G. Abbot, 'Shanti' Stone. Behind the wheel: A. Howard, M. Howard. Back row: Only the right hand man is known: E. Kingham.

To the Shops

ABOVE: Mr & Mrs Pratt outside their Church Street confectionery, and BELOW: Mr Hoar stands between his staff, Co-op butchers, High Street.

LEFT: Long Bros put on a display in Broad Street. RIGHT: Wrights have survived in Germain Street, but BELOW: Goss's Tea Rooms have not; nor has The House of Tree; Chesham Estate Office remains, a few doors up in The Broadway. (W)

ABOVE: Mr How reflected the town's brush wares in High Street, (now Kim and Gay's),while BELOW: Mr Young's emporium (now Gutteridge's), was watched over by a parrot who greeted customers on entry.

In the News

ABOVE: Churchgoers gather for a fete in The Bury. (W) CENTRE: The walking race for senior citizens. (W) BELOW: The ladies have a go in the egg and spoon event. (W)

ABOVE: Carnival floats are nothing new — here in Bellingdon Road. (W) BELOW: An early church outing, out of town.

INSET: Garden Party. (W) ABOVE: Carnival Procession. (W) BELOW: The Royal and Ancient Order of Buffaloes off for an outing. (B)

Riverside

ABOVE: A clean river Chess at Waterside. BELOW: Water Lane, near the Town Bridge looking towards Church Street from Germain Street, Wright's timber yard in the background. (W)

ABOVE: Boating down the river off The Moor, near New Road. The bridge is still there. (W) BELOW: Duck Alley for a ducking — off Germain Street. (W)

ABOVE: Quiet flows the Chess by The Moor, (W) and BELOW:
Lord's Mill on the river — source of the town's original industry.

Breathing Space

ABOVE: The avenue of elms that once lined the road through the Park, with BELOW: cattle watering where the town plays today.

ABOVE: Jolly boating weather. The elms went in 1950. BELOW: End of an afternoon on Skottowe's Pond.

ABOVE: A last look at the elm avenue. BELOW: The Grove at The Bury — an oasis on the Chess.

Town at Heart

ABOVE: Gypsies bring the fair to town — in The Broadway, (W) while BELOW: they camped behind The Rink, off Red Lion Street — Maisie makes her daughter smart. (W)

ABOVE: Gaslight and gowns in The Broadway, c1905; CENTRE: the unlamented Lamb public house dominates the opposite view, and BELOW: a hot day with the blinds down as the Rover 'bus enters High Street.

ABOVE: The other end of High Street, looking towards Berkhamsted, jay walking permitted. BELOW: Newspapers delivered, parking space galore, and gardens behind the Red Lion, corner of Market Square and Germain Street.

ABOVE: Dray delivery to the Crown (now Tesco) and Market Hall — since overtaken by the ubiquitous car. BELOW: Duck Alley, with the old sweet shop.

ABOVE: Quiet corner of Church Street. BELOW: Fuller's Hill winds out of town.

Let's Play

ABOVE: Chesham Scout Troop had the only trumpet band within 50 miles of London: they appeared in the Lord Mayor's Show. Here on January 19, 1918 they leave Christ Church, Waterside, after service. Scoutmaster Hart leads; lead drummer Reginald Howard and lead trumpeter Jack Hearn nearest camera. (H) BELOW: Chesham Amateur Operatic and Dramatic Society's 1924 *Mikado;* L-R: Harold Green, Dorry Hanks, Maggie Webb, Bert Batchelor. (BB)

ABOVE: Chesham Generals were Spartan League Champions 1913-14. Team only — R. Stephenson, A. Reynolds, C. Webb. A. Thorne, F. Birch, W. Keen, F. Newman, W. Bolton, A. Moulder, A. Sawyer, F. Thompson, W. Richardson, J. King. (L) BELOW: Chesham United FC second team were Chesham League (Div 1) and Spartan League (Div 2) cupwinners in 1921-22. J. Humphrey (trainer), H. Redding, C. Webb (Capt), S. Ringsell, A. Moulder (team manager), H. Lacey (Hon Sec), M. Barnes, E. Woolford, J. Rogers, A. Rogers, F. Filby, G. Hammond, A. Wright, C. Rance, S. Rance.

ABOVE: United's A team, 1927-28, pride of Chesham's football-conscious crowds. BELOW: Chesham Cricket Club. (B)

Sunday Best

ABOVE: The town turns out for George V's Jubilee, 1935. BELOW: Wesleyan Sunday Scholars' (est 1888) flower festival in Broad Street.

ABOVE: The Buffaloes mount a 'wedding' as a Christian act for the hospital charity. (B) BELOW: Hinton draws the crowds and a fine carriage for the real thing. (W)

Here comes the bride. (W)

St Mary's Parish Church — where the town began, the story ends.
(W)

Day's End

Picture Index

KEY TO CAPTION CREDITS

W Augustus Writer, by courtesy of Enid Desborough, Babs Rowland, Beryl Brandon and Derek Writer
G By courtesy of Frank Gomm
S By courtesy of Mrs F. M. Smith
H By courtesy of Reginald F. Howard
A By courtesy of Grace Auchterlonie
M By courtesy of Chesham & District Mutual Building Society
B By courtesy of Mrs B. Bristow
L By courtesy of Mrs L. Moulder
C By courtesy of Mrs Cancel
D Charles Darvell
MH Michael Howard
BB Bert Batchelor
WTM Will Moulder

All other material from photographs from many sources collected by the author or John Armistead

---

Clive Birch lived in Chesham for a quarter of a century. Born in 1931 and educated at Uppingham School, he was Editor of the *Bucks Examiner* in the '50s and at one time Editor and Director of *The Illustrated London News*. He has written or co-authored *The Book of Chesham, Yesterday's Town: Chesham, The Book of Aylesbury, The Book of Amersham* and *The Book of Beaconsfield;* he edited and designed *Maps of Bucks*. He lives at Radclive near Buckingham.

John Armistead was born in 1938, and has lived in Chesham, where he now works in the engineering industry, since 1943. Photography is his hobby and he has worked with Clive Birch on all his books, co-authoring *Yesterday's Town: Chesham*.

Augustus Writer, whose photographs form the majority in this volume, lived and worked in Chesham from 1913 to his death in 1943. Of his four surviving children, three still live in the town.

Barracuda Books was founded in Chesham and published all the local volumes listed above. Altogether fifty seven Town Books, four Yesterday's Towns, and a number of railway, church and family histories now form this unique collection of local books. (Meadows House, Well Street, Buckingham.)

Clive Birch

John Armistead

Augustus Writer